I0021957

Cloud Security

Introduction to cloud security and data protection

Nate Jenner

Copyright © 2018 by Nate Jenner

All rights reserved. No part of this publication may be reproduced, distributed, or transmitted in any form or by any means, including photocopying, recording, or other electronic or mechanical methods, without the prior written permission of the author, except in the case of brief quotations embodied in critical reviews and certain other noncommercial uses permitted by copyright law.

Table of Contents

Introduction

Organizations need cheap and flexible way of storing data. They are a in off-site storages if possible so in need of a simple way through which they can share data with other organizations as well as with individuals. The cloud is the only way through which organizations can achieve this. The cloud is ubiquitous, in that it can be accessed at any time, by any authorized entity and using any device. The cloud also scales well to meet an increase in the demand for storage space. However, despite the many benefits associated with the cloud, it faces a security challenge. Many incidences have been reported of hackers gaining access to the cloud and stealing, modifying or even deleting user data. Organizations and cloud service providers should implement better strategies to deal with this. This book helps you understand the threats facing cloud security and the measures you can put into place to ensure that the cloud is secure.

Chapter 1- What is Cloud Security?

Cloud computing security is nowadays one of the fastest growing services with functionalities related to those of IT security. It involves the protection of critical information from theft, deletion or data leakage. The good thing with the cloud is that you can operate at scale while at the same time remaining secure. In cloud security, we employ similar approaches used in IT security including preventive, detective and corrective measures. However, in cloud security, these activities can be done in a more agile manner.

Due to the nature of the cloud, that is, it is a shared resource; there is a need to implement proper measures for identity management, privacy and access control. Cloud computing security measures should address all security controls that a cloud provider will incorporate in order to maintain the security, privacy and compliance of the customer data with the necessary regulations. Cloud computing security measures should also include plans for business continuity and data backup so that the organization can be in a position to continue with its operations in case of occurrence of a security breach. The cloud is a very accessible service. It is ubiquitous as it is accessed by users using various devices.

These users are also connecting to the cloud from various locations in the world. Some organizations keep much of their sensitive data in the cloud, meaning that in case of a serious security breach, the organization operations can be crippled. Cloud security should be taken with a lot of seriousness. This is not the role of a single individual or company, but all individuals accessing and using the cloud have an active role to play as far as cloud security is concerned.

Chapter 2- Cloud Security Threats, Risks and Concerns

In most companies, the cloud computing and cloud security go hand-in-hand. The use of a public cloud is a cheap way of storing data for any organization, but it can at the same time introduce some new risks if proper protection measures are not put into place. There are various threats, risks and concerns about cloud security. Let us discuss them.

Data Breaches

Cloud environments normally implement some security measures, but they face the same challenges as the traditional networks. In case a data breach occurs, sensitive information such as credit card data, trade secrets and intellectual property can be exposed, which can lead to serious consequences. Example, companies may face hefty fines and lawsuits, or even damage the image of the brand which could last for several years. Reputable cloud services rely on numerous security protocols for protection of sensitive information. However, your organization should come up with a way of protecting the sensitive data they have kept in the cloud. Multifactor authentication and encryption are the best ways to ensure that sensitive data in the cloud is secure. A user may use a virtual machine to listen to an activity that indicates the arrival of an encryption key on another virtual machine running on the same host. This way, sensitive data for an organization can fall into the hands of enemies and competitors. In case the organization had kept some sensitive data in the cloud and a security breach occurs, then it may have to notify and alert the potential victims. This is what majority of regulations especially the ones in health care sector require. After a breach disclosure, regulators may levy fines against the company, while consumers whose information has been exposed may file lawsuits.

Data Loss

A data breach normally results from a malicious and most probably an intrusive activity.

If a disk drive at a time when the owner had not created its backup, this will result into a data loss. If you own some encrypted data, then you lose the key that unlocks the data, then data loss will occur. In a malicious attack occurs, a data loss may occur, an intentional data loss may occur.

The possibility of an individual or a company losing all the data they have kept in the cloud is minimal. However, cases have been reported of hackers who have gained access to the cloud data centers and wiped out all the data for a company or individual. This explains the importance of distributing your applications across numerous zones and backing up your data in off-site storage if possible.

There is a need for you to understand the compliance policies governing what you are allowed to do and what you are not allowed to do with collected data. This will help you know how to stay protected in case a data breach occurs so that you don't fall into trouble. If a data loss occurs, customers will lose confidence with you. They will look for services elsewhere, and this will lead to loss of revenue.

Hijacked Accounts

Activities such as exploitation of software vulnerabilities like buffer overflow attacks, phishing, loss of passwords and other credentials can lead to loss of control over the affected user account. An intruder who gains control over an account can manipulate data, eavesdrop on transactions, redirect customers to inappropriate or competitors' site or even provide responses to customers to damage the business.

In case the affected account had been connected to several other accounts, it is easy for you to lose control over them. By choosing a unique and secure password for an account, you can prevent numerous security threats. If you are running multiple accounts, it may be hard for you to manage their passwords.

However, a password manager can help in making your work easier. You can also implement a multifactor authentication mechanism to prevent attackers from gaining access to such accounts.

Denial of Service (DOS) Attacks

In case of occurrence of a DOS attack, the operations of your organization can be crippled. Such attacks have been a threat to computer network for numerous years. With cloud computing, these attacks have become more prevalent. DOS attacks consume a lot of processing power; hence they have a direct effect on the speed and availability of the cloud services. In case a DOS attack occurs, there is nothing you can do, but just to relax and wait. The attack may bring in an additional load, which you have to pay for, if the attack is severe, financial losses may occur. The DOS attacks are an old technique that targets online transactions, but they are still a threat today. The attacker sends thousands of requests to the server, tying up transactions. Such attacks affect the availability of services offered to an organization by the cloud. If the DOS attacks become persistent, it may become hard for you to run your service, and you may be forced to take it down.

Hacked APIs an Interfaces

In most cloud services, applications rely on APIs for communication with other cloud services. Due to this, the security of the API has a direct impact as far as the security of the cloud is concerned. In case a third party is granted access to the API, then the chances of the API getting hacked increases. In some cases, the organization may end up losing sensitive data pertaining its customers. When using the cloud, there is a contradiction in providing millions of services to the connecting customers while at the same time ensuring that you limit the damage that may be brought by these customers, most of whom are anonymous users. The security of the API should be considered as early as during the development of the same. This way, it will be easy to implement threat modeling systems and applications to thwart such attacks.

Malicious Insiders

Malicious insiders are a threat to cloud security. In case there is one in a giant cloud organization, then the threat becomes magnified.

One of the ways through such cloud users can stay safe from this is by keeping their encryption keys on their premises rather than in the cloud. Research has shown that a system that relies on the cloud for security is at a higher risk.

Abusing Cloud Services

Cloud computing provides elastic, large-scale services to the enterprise users as well as hackers. It is always cheap to deploy an infrastructure, which means that it is trivial to carry out an attack, from the perspective of cost. While a limited hardware, an attacker may spend years in trying to crack an encryption key. However, the same can be accomplished in minutes when using cloud servers. Hackers may also use cloud servers for serving malware, distributing malware software or launching DDOS attacks.

The service providers are responsible for the control of the use of the cloud service, but the question is, how are able to detect inappropriate uses? Is there a clear definition of what an abuse is? In case it occurs once, how can it be prevented in the future?

Cloud customers normally assess various cloud providers based on these in order to choose the one who can respond well.

Lack of Due Diligence

Due diligence refers to the process of evaluating various cloud providers in a bid to ensure that best practices are put into place. This also involves evaluating the level of security that the cloud provider can offer to its customers and meet the level of service that the enterprise expects. If a customer doesn't understand the protection and environment offered by the service provider, you will not know what to expect for an incident response, security monitoring and encryption use.

This way, the organization will take unknown levels of risk even in ways they cannot comprehend. This means that there will be variation between what the customers expect and what the service provider can offer.

The customer will not even know the liability to expect from the provider in any case a security breach occurs.

Weak Identity and Authentication Management Systems

Lack of strong authentication and identity management systems has led to the occurrence of security breaches in most organizations. Businesses normally face a challenge in implementing identity management procedures, especially in assigning permissions that correspond to the job role of the user.

A good example of a breach that resulted from this is Anthem Inc. data breach that was orchestrated using lost credentials, leading to illegal access to 80 million records with personal and medical information. A multifactor authentication could have helped thwart this attack if it had been put into place.

Weak identity management can cause loopholes in the system of an organization. Even if a password for logging into a cloud account is lost, it is possible for you to prevent any person with the person from logging into the account. A multifactor authentication system such as one-time password (OTP) can help in such a case.

Chapter 3- Cloud Security Controls

Cloud security controls are set of controls that enable cloud architecture to offer protection against vulnerabilities or reduce or mitigate the effects of a malicious attack. It consists of all practices, measures and guidelines that must be implemented for protection of a cloud computing environment. Cloud security control helps in evaluating, addressing and implementing security in a cloud environment. Below are the security controls that every organization should implement to ensure its cloud data is safe and secure:

1. Security Architecture. The organization must consider the security of the whole stack that delivers the service, from the physical hardware including how it is secured, to the network (firewall rules etc.), virtual machines and the application. No part of the cloud or the organization should be left unsecured; otherwise, you are exposing your data to hackers.

2. Identity and Access Management. A good cloud solution should have a clear identification and authorization framework. Such a framework is normally referred to as 3As, which stands for Authentication, Authorization and Access Control. The cloud service provider is required to provide single sign-on capabilities. Hackers are using new and sophisticated attack techniques each day. With a multifactor authentication scheme, such attacks can be thwarted. For example, a user may be required to enter a password plus a one-time-password (OTP) that will be sending to their handheld device like a mobile phone. The generated OTP should be set to expire after some few minutes, after which the user will require to request for a new one to be generated. For the hacker to gain access to the cloud user account, they require the password and physical access to the mobile device.

3. Data Protection. Data security involves protecting the data across the entire lifecycle of the data, beginning from the creation of the data to when the cloud service provider destroys the data if you leave their platform. Encryption is very important, and it should be employed in all data lifecycle steps.

4. Governance. In the cloud paradigm, the organization exercises direct control over many aspects of data and security,

making governance a key since it provides control and visibility over procedures, policies and standards for development and implementation of applications and continuous monitoring of applications and services that have been deployed to the cloud.

5. Risk Management. Cloud service providers are expected to provide a robust framework for risk assessment, and this should include reports about vulnerability scans, dynamic and static application security testing as well as other tools for risk assessment. All organizations are advised to check on what should go to the cloud and what should not. Example, it may be not good for data and files with sensitive information to go to the cloud, example, mission critical content, intellectual property, regulated data etc.

6. Compliance. Compliance refers to conformance with the established specification, regulation, standard or law. The compliance requirements in this case can be based on your industry, location of the cloud data center that your company is using or on your geographical location. Organization should always get complete audit reports of their data, users and devices in a bid to stay on the top of compliance all the time.

Chapter 4- Identity and Access Management

Majority of companies are adding cloud services to their IT environments which is making the process of identity management more complex. In any system, security involves ensuring that each entity gets access to the right data, in an authorized format and at the authorized time and from a location that is authorized. To implement Identity and Access Management (IAM) in an organization, there is a need for the organization and the cloud service provider to maintain an audit trail for all events from logging to the system, authentication and accessing files and running applications as authorized.

IAM can be said to be the best security model for any cloud. This explains the reason as why a cloud service provides like AWS (Amazon Web Services) provides IAM to its customers as service out of box. In other cloud service providers, you are required to select and deploy some third party IAM systems like Okta and Ping Identity.

IAM Functions

1. Identity Management. Identity management should involve authenticating users and determining whether they will be permitted to access certain systems. Management and identity access management goes hand in hand. Management involves authentication, while access management involves authorization.

The purpose of identity management is to determine whether a user is allowed to access systems, while at the same time setting the level of access and permissions that the user has on the particular system. With such a mechanism, a user may be granted access to a particular system, but some of its components or features may be hidden from the user.

Identity management should ensure that only the authenticated users are granted access to specific applications, systems or IT environments for which they have been authorized. This also involves control over user provisioning and on boarding new users like partners, employees, clients as well as other stakeholders. Identity management also involves the process of authorization of system or network permissions for the existing users and off boarding users who are not authorized any longer to access the organization systems.

2. Identity Governance. Governance is also an important part of identity management. It involves administering the processes and policies that guide how the users and roles access systems and applications across the business environment. Identity governance is very essential in successfully managing role-based access management systems. Identity management is very essential to any organization since it plays a great role in both the security and productivity of the organization. In most organizations, it has been found that users are granted many access privileges than the functions that they need to perform. Hackers can take advantage of compromised user credentials to gain access to data and network for the organization. By use of identity management, organizations are capable of safeguarding their corporate assets against threats such as ransomware, hacking, phishing as well as other malware attacks.

With identity management, you can add a protection layer by ensuring that user access rules and policies are consistently applied across the entire organization.

With an identity and access management system, you can provide a framework that will include the technology and policies that are needed to support the process of managing digital and electronic identities. Majority of IAM systems of today rely on federated identity so that they can be authenticated then stored across many disparate systems.

3. Single Sign-On (SSO). With an IAM system, it is easy for an organization to implement single sign-on (SSO) technologies so that we may reduce the number of passwords that are needed. SSO uses a federated-identity approach by use of a single login and password in order to create some authentication token that may be accepted by different enterprise systems and applications. When this is combined with multifactor authentication and enforceable security policies like the principle of the least privilege, which provides users with only the access they require in order to fulfill their roles, enterprises will be in a position to lower the risk of breaches.

4. Authorization Management. Most organizations of all sizes have requirements that govern the authorization of users to use the cloud-based services. This includes assigning rights to the employees based on the position they hold in the company. In other cases, the application may need the implementation of Role-Based Access Control (RBAC), but the cloud-based authorization system may be unable to provide security at this level. This has a direct consequence in that the services provided in the cloud will not be able to respond to the requirements that have been established within the organization. In most organizations, two types of roles are provided, that is, the *administrator* and *user* roles. In such a case, the administrator role has full privileges in user authentication and security policies statement areas.

5. Compliance Management. The architecture and practices for identity and access management in a cloud environment have an essential role in overall assessment of effectiveness of business processes in the organization. This makes them very important for the purpose of managing compliance. For example, if we automate the process of granting and withdrawing access rights, organizations attain the capability of reducing any unauthorized access from happening.

Challenges to Implementation of Identity Management Practices

For an organization to be capable of implementing good and effective identity management practices, the organization should have the capability of planning and collaborating across the business units. Organizations that set identity management practices with defined business processes and clear objectives will have high chances of success. For identity management to work well, security, IT and human resource should be combined. Other departments should also be involved as well.

The identity management systems should be capable of allowing users to manage multiple users using different computing environments in a real time manner. It is not feasible for any organization to manually adjust the access controls and access privileges for thousands of users.

It should also be easy for users to perform authentication, and easy for the IT staff to deploy and manage it.

A big challenge in implementing identity management is password management. The process of creating, updating and even deleting passwords may be costly, and the organization may need reducing such costs. The IT staff should look for ways to reduce the effect of such password issues on the organization.

Tools for managing the identity management should run in the form of an application on some dedicated server or network appliance, either on the cloud or on the premises. In an identity management system, there are policies that define the devices and users are allowed to access the network and what they can accomplish, based on the type of the device, its location and several other factors. This is also determined by the appropriate management console functionality, such as policy definition, alerts, reports, alarms and other operation and management requirements.

The organization may consider implementing an alarm that will ring whenever a user tries to access a resource for which they are not allowed to access. The reporting feature will provide an audit of the specific activities that have taken place.

Majority of identity management systems provide directory integration and support for both wireless and wired users, and flexibility to meet any operational and security policy requirement. Since BYOD (Bring Your Own Device) has become so strategic today, time-saving features like automated device provisioning and on boarding, automated device status verification and support for many mobile operating systems are becoming very common.

Chapter 5- Data Security and Privacy

Data security has been a major concern in IT. In cloud computing environment, the data is kept in different locations. Every cloud user is concerned about the security and privacy of their data. Both the hardware and the software used in a cloud environment play a significant role as far as the security and privacy of data is concerned. Let us discuss the data attributes and properties that should be protected in the cloud and how to protect them.

Data Integrity

Data integrity is an important part in any information system. Data integrity is the process of protecting data from unauthorized deletion, fabrication or modification. It also involves the management of admittance of an entity as well as management of access rights to various resources of the enterprise to ensure that valuable services and data are not abused, stolen or misappropriated.

For the case of a standalone system running a single database, it is easy to implement and manage data integrity. Database constraints and transactions are used to implement data integrity in such an environment. This is normally done via the database management system (DBMS) itself.

In a cloud environment, data integrity involves protecting the integrity of information. The data shouldn't be modified or lost by an unauthorized user. Data integrity is verified essential when it comes to provision of cloud computing services like PaaS, SaaS and IaaS. Other than the storage of large-scaled data, the cloud computing environment provides service for data processing. The integrity of data can be achieved through techniques like digital signature and RAID.

The cloud computing has numerous access points and there are many entities in need of accessing its services. Due to this, authorization is very essential to help ensure that only the authorized entities are allowed to interact with the data. If unauthorized access is prevented, organizations will gain much confidence as far as data integrity is concerned.

Monitoring mechanisms provide a greater way of determining who or what might have changed the system information which could have affected the integrity. The cloud computing providers are in most cases left with the responsibility of maintaining the integrity of data kept in the cloud. It is also possible for one to create a third-party mechanism other than the cloud service provider and the users. The process of verifying the integrity of data stored in the cloud is perquisite to deployment of applications.

Data Confidentiality

Data confidentiality is very essential for the users who keep their data in the cloud. Access control and authentication strategies are implemented in a bid to ensure that data is kept confidentially. The authentication, access control and confidentiality issues in a cloud computing environment can be avoided by increasing the trustworthiness and reliability of using the cloud.

Since most users do not most cloud providers and the cloud service providers are virtually impossible of eliminating the potential insider threat, it becomes dangerous when users directly keep their sensitive data in the cloud. The use of simple encryption is faced by the challenge of key management and it cannot support complex requirements like parallel modification, query and fine-grained authorization.

Homomorphic Encryption

Encryption is highly used for data confidentiality. Homomorphic encryption ensures that cipher text algebraic operation results remain consistent with clear operation after the encryption results, and the whole process doesn't have to decrypt the data.

Implementation of such a technique can help in solving the problem of data operations and data confidentiality in the cloud. A fully homormophic encryption method capable of doing any operation that may be performed in clear text with no decryption. This is a great achievement in the homormophic encryption technologies.

However, this encryption process involves a very complicated circulation, making the cost of computation and storage very high. This means that this encryption process is still far from being applied in real life applications. Diffie-Hellman, a cryptography algorithm is proposed for use in secure communication. This algorithm works similar to what happens in the key distribution mechanism. For enhanced security and flexibility, a hybrid approach that utilizes multiple encryption algorithms like 3DES, RSA and random number generator is recommended. With RSA, a secure communication can be established through authentication via digital signature. 3DES algorithm is only suitable for encryption of a block data.

Encrypted Search and Database

Due to the inefficiency of the homormophic encryption algorithm, researchers are now studying how the limited homomorphic encryption algorithm can be applied to a cloud environment.

Encrypted search is a popular operation. A lightweight mechanism for encryption of a database has been proposed, and this is referred to as transposition, substitution, folding, and shifting (TSFS) algorithm. However, with the increase in the number of keys, the amount of processing and computations also increases.

For organizations that use an entrusted cloud computing environment, the use of in-memory database encryption technique is recommended for security and privacy of private data. There is a synchronizer between the client and the owner for seeking access to data. The client will need a key from the synchronizer in order to decrypt the shared encrypted data that it receives from the owner. The synchronizer stores the keys and the correlated shared data separately. This technique has a problem in that due to the additional communication with central synchronizer leads to delays. This problem can be mitigated via adoption of group encryption and reduction of the communication between the synchronizer and the nodes.

A mechanism for asymmetric encryption of databases in the cloud has also been recommended.

A cumulative encryption will be applied to data for more than once during which the order in which the public/private key is used will not matter.

A re-encryption mechanism will also be used for showing that the cipher-text data has been encrypted once again for duality purposes. Such schemes become very useful in a cloud environment where there are concerns about privacy.

Distributive Storage

Distributive storage of data in the cloud is also a good way of ensuring there is security and privacy of data. As a way of ensuring that there is data integrity, it is recommended that we store data in various cloud databases or multiple clouds. The data that needs to be protected against internal or external unauthorized access is first divided into chunks, then Shamir's secret algorithm is applied in order to generate a polynomial function for each chunk.

Hybrid Technique

This is a technique that has been proposed for data privacy and integrity and it uses both authentication and key sharing techniques. The RSA public key algorithm should then be used for a secure distribution of the keys between the cloud service providers and the users. It is recommended that a three-layered data security technique should be used.

In the first layer, the cloud user should be authenticated via a one factor of multifactor authentication. In the second layer, the user should be encrypted for privacy and protection of the data. The third layer, a speedy decryption process should be done to facilitate a fast recovery of the data. The critical data kept in the cloud should also be isolated via an event-driven data isolation technique. TrustDraw can be used, which is a transparent security extension for the cloud combining trusted computing (TC) and virtual machine introspection (VMI).

Data Concealment

This is a good technique to ensure there is confidentiality of data in the cloud.

Most data concealment approaches involve merging the real data with visual fake data in order to falsify the volume of the real data. However, it is easy for authorized users to separate the real data from the fake data. With data concealment techniques, the volume of the real data is increased while proving an enhanced security for private data. With data concealment, the real data can be made safe and secure from malicious users. The watermarking method can also be used for securing such data. Only the authorized users will have the watermarking key.

Deletion Confirmation

Deletion confirmation is an indication that data cannot be recovered once the users have deleted their data. However, there is a problem with this. There are multiple copies in the cloud kept for security purposes. If a user confirms the deletion, then all of these will be deleted. However, there are technologies that can be used for recovery of the data from the hard disks. The cloud service provider should ensure that the data deleted by users cannot be recovered and users by users who are not authenticated.

A good of preventing this is by encrypting the data before it can be uploaded to the cloud. You can use technologies that are based on FADE like Ephemerizer. These systems encrypt data before it is uploaded to the storage.

Data Availability

Cloud users should be capable of accessing their data even after occurrence of an incidence in the cloud. The cloud users should be aware of the rules that govern the availability of data in the cloud. The following are some techniques that can be employed that cloud data is available to its users:

Reliable Storage Agreement

In some cases, the update data from a user may be discarded by the cloud provider when using an entrusted storage and it may be hard to check this when relying on a simple encryption technique. A good storage management is the one that supports concurrent updates to be done by users.

In such a case, consistency is a very important aspect.

Hard-Drive Reliability

The hard drive is used as the main storage media in the cloud. How reliable the hard drive is determining the foundation of the cloud storage. Cloud providers need to ensure that they the hard drives they use for storage are reliable in order to increase user's confidence in the cloud service.

Data Privacy

Privacy refers to the ability of a group or an individual to seclude them or information about themselves and reveal it selectively. In the cloud environment, once a user visits some sensitive data, the cloud service should be capable of preventing a potential adversary from inferring the behavior of the user from their visit model;

Researchers have recommended the oblivious RAM (ORAM) technology. The ORAM technology works by visiting numerous data copies to hide the visiting aims of the users. This technique has widely been used in software protection as well as protecting privacy in the cloud, and it seems to be very promising. The following are some malpractices in the cloud that can be done in the cloud to compromise data privacy and how to thwart such:

Service Abuse

This occurs when attackers abuse the cloud service and get extra data or destroy the interests of other users. Some users may abuse the data of other users. The cloud storage has relied on the reduplication technology for a long time, meaning that the same data was stored once but shared amongst various users. This reduces storage space and cuts down cloud service provider expenses, but if the hackers are aware of the hash code of the stored data, they will be able to access the data. Sensitive cloud data may then be leaked in the process. This is why it is recommended that the proof of ownership approach be used for checking the authenticity of cloud users.

Attackers may increase of using the cloud service. This is as a result of a fraudulent use of a cloud service.

Averting Attacks

In the cloud environment, there are numerous shared resources. The cloud system should be capable of preventing the DO (Denial of Service) attacks. To thwart this, it is recommended that there should be integration for trusted computing platform (TCP) with trusted platform support services (TSS). The trusted model must have characteristics of dynamic of services, confidentiality and dynamically building trust domains. The cloud infrastructures expect the users to transfer their data to the cloud based on trust.

Identity Management

The cloud provides its users with a place where they can use a number of internet-based services. The use of a trusted third party in the cloud increases the security threat. When a third party is used, there are high chances of having heterogeneous users, and this affects the security of the cloud service. The solution to this problem is by use of trusted third-party independent approach, so that identity management may be able to use identity data in entrusted hosts.

Chapter 6- Incident Response

Although you might have put numerous security practices into place, a security breach may occur in a cloud environment. In such an occurrence, the cloud service provider and the users should respond appropriately to alleviate any further damages to their cloud data and further losses. Every cloud service provider should maintain a well-defined plan dictating the steps that the incident response team will follow in case a security breach occurs.

The following are the steps that should be followed in case a security breach occurs in the cloud:

1. Preparation. Preparation is very essential for an effective incident response. Without a set of predetermined guidelines, it will be hard for a response team to do their work effectively. The incidence response plan should define the necessary incident response policies as well as the associated procedures and agreements. Communication guidelines should also be created to ensure a proper communication during and after the incident. The incident response team should conduct exercise which will help them know the incidents which are happening in the environment. You should also assess your ability to respond to events and make any necessary improvements.

2. Detection and Reporting. In this step, the incident response team has to monitor the security events so as detect, alert then report any potential security incidences.

The monitoring of the security events is done using intrusion prevention systems, firewalls and data loss prevention.

3. Containment and Neutralization. This is a very critical stage in an incident response process. The strategy used for containment and neutralization of the threats is determined by the intelligence and the gathered which was gathered during the analysis phase. Once the security is verified and the system restored, the normal operations can be resumed.

A coordinated shutdown may be needed once all the systems which have been compromised by the threat actor are identified. All these systems are shut down, and notifications must be sending to the incident response team members to ensure there is a coordinated timing.

The infected devices can be wiped and the operating system rebuild from ground up. Passwords for all the compromised accounts should be changed.

In case you identify IP addresses and domains which come from threat actors, give threat mitigation requests for communications from these to be blocked.

4. Post-Incident Tasks. Once the issue has been solved, there is still much to be done. If you identify any information which can be used for mitigation of similar attacks in the future, just document them. The incident should be documented well so that the incident response plan can be improved and take any security measures for prevention of such incidents from occurring in the future.

Even after the incident, you should continue monitoring the activities since the threat actors will appear again. You can use a security log and hawk through it to analyze the data and check whether there are signs of any attack on your systems. New measures also need to be created to prevent any attacks in the future.

The Incident Response Team

Both the cloud service provider and the organization using the cloud for storage of data should have established incident response team. The team should be made up of individuals with good skills and experience in computer and cloud security. With such a team especially in the cloud service provider, it will not only be possible to respond appropriately to cloud security breaches, but also detect the threats and thwart them early in advance.

The following are the core members of the incident response team:

1. Incident Response Manager. He is responsible for overseeing and prioritizing actions during detection, analysis and the containment of the incident. The Incident Response Manager is also responsible for communicating the special requirements of the high severity incidents to the company members.

2. Security Analysts. The manger works together with a team of security analysts who work directly with the network to find

the location, time and other details in case a network attack incident occurs. The following are the various types of analysts:

- Triage Analysts- these are responsible for filtering our false positives and watching for potential intrusions.
- Forensic Analysts- these are responsible for recovering key artifacts and maintaining the integrity of evidence to ensure there is a forensically sound investigation.

3. Threat Researchers. These provide threat intelligence and context for the incident to compliment the efforts of the security analysts. They constantly combine the internet and identify intelligence which might have been reported externally. When this information is combined with the company records regarding the previous incidences, a database of internal intelligence can be building and maintained. With such a team, response to security breaches in the cloud will be done in the appropriate way.

Chapter 7- Challenges to Cloud Security

The cloud provides its users with a way of storing their data and accessing from heterogeneous devices. However, this comes with greater security risks. The clouding is nowadays becoming an integral part in business processes. Organizations are relying on the cloud to provide services to their remote users. However, due to the use of multiple data centers, devices, networks and users who are issued with varying access rights, cloud security has become very complex and a challenge. An increase in the use of the cloud is marked by an increase in the number. The cloud comes with some unique security challenges like an increase in the devices accessing the network. Traditional security measures are not well-equipped to handle such challenges.

Risky App Usage

The increase in the use of the cloud applications has made life easier on the part of the users. A lot of data is being exchanged across such applications. However, this has a problem in that the organization is put at a higher risk due to the security loopholes in such apps. Research has shown that an average organization uses about 928 cloud applications. However, CIOs in most organizations are only aware of 40 of such applications. The organizations and the cloud are at risk due to the security loopholes in the rest of the applications that are being used. The apps for the organizations should be protected from security threats like DDOS, SQL Injection and other such attacks. This can be achieved by application-level security like server firewalls. These will help in defining how applications will be used and how the data may be viewed.

Cyber Conflicts and Advanced Attacks

Cloud attackers are become more complex every day and the threat actors are becoming sophisticated. The threat actors are constantly looking for ways to overcome the security mechanisms that are implemented in the cloud. Note that the cloud service provider needs to close every loophole that the potential attackers may use to gain access into the systems.

At the same time, an attacker only needs to identity a single loophole, however weak it might be to gain access to the stored data. Such a loophole can be escalated to even shutdown the cloud system. The best way to avoid this is through encryption. Organizations have realized that data encryption is one of the ways to reduce the risk to which the data is exposed.

System Vulnerabilities

System vulnerabilities and bugs can be a great challenge in the cloud, especially in a shared cloud environment. If for example users leave a system in its default configuration setting, it may be prone to a ransomware attack. To solve system vulnerabilities, you only have to use basic IT processes like patching, scanning and do up on the reported system threats. The system activity should be monitored regularly as well as the logs in order to assess the level of risk.

Insecure Access Points

One of the characteristics of the cloud is that it is accessible from any device and from any location. What will happen if the interfaces and APIs that users interact with are not secure? It will become possible for hackers to identify such weaknesses and exploit them. A behavioral web application firewall is capable of examining HTTP requests to a website in order to ensure that the traffic is legitimate. With such an always-on device, web applications can be protected against security breaches.

Securing Sensitive Data

A research has shown that 62% of companies keep their data in a public cloud while 40% of companies begin using cloud services without consulting their IT department. This makes such organizations susceptible to data breaches and lawsuits, fines and damaged public reputation in any case a security breach occurs. Cloud providers normally deploy security controls in order to protect their environments, but the role of protecting data lies solely to the organizations. Encryption and multifactor authentication should be employed as the best ways of protecting the data.

The data should be encrypted when it is stored and when it is being transmitted. Approved encryption algorithms and long encryption keys should be used. The data should also be encrypted before it can move from the enterprise to the cloud provider. Organizations are also discouraged from giving the decryption keys to the cloud provider or its staff. Overlooked files such as metadata and logs should be protected.

Vulnerabilities in APIs and App Code

The way in which cloud services are designed may also be a challenge in implementing security practices.

The code and API for an app define how secure it is. In the cloud, most of the apps are designed with usability under consideration, not security. This means that an app can be well functional, but it could have numerous security vulnerabilities. When third parties build on these APIs and apps, the security increases further. This calls for all apps from vendors to be reviewed to determine how secure they are.

Shadow IT

Businesses are growing at an exponential rate. However, they are bypassing IT and its security regulations, which can in turn put them at a bigger security threat. Although this is a good way of doing things faster, it exposes the organization and its data at a security risk.

To prevent data from leaking as a result of shadow IT, businesses are advised to encrypt their data and implement an intelligent model for key management. With key management, they can regulate how encrypted data is accessed so that access can only be granted to those whose work needs to use the data. For the case of managing the key, the organization may choose to manage the key on their own, or they can choose to let the cloud service provider to manage the key.

Conclusion

Most organizations are moving their data to the cloud. This is because the cloud provides a cheap of storing and sharing data between individuals and organizations. Organizations should consider the security of the data that they store in the cloud. Multiple users are accessing the cloud data. These users are connecting to the cloud from different locations in the world, at various times and using heterogeneous devices. Each of these devices has its own security loopholes, which hackers can take advantage of to steal the cloud data. The best way to ensure cloud data is safe is by encrypting the data and using multifactor authentication.

www.ingramcontent.com/pod-product-compliance
Lightning Source LLC
Chambersburg PA
CBHW070906070326
40690CB00009B/2023